WORLD
CULTURES
in Perspective

Southeast Asian
Cultures
IN PERSPECTIVE

Don Nardo

Mitchell Lane
PUBLISHERS
P.O. Box 196
Hockessin, Delaware 19707

WORLD CULTURES in Perspective

Printing   1   2   3   4   5   6   7   8   9

Library of Congress Cataloging-in-Publication Data
Nardo, Don, 1947– author.
  Southeast Asian cultures in perspective / by Don Nardo.
        pages cm. — (World cultures in perspective)
  Includes bibliographical references and index.
  Summary: "Southeast Asian Cultures in Perspective is an in-depth look at the
different regional cultures of Southeast Asia with an emphasis on current culture.
The young reader is presented with an overview of a variety of regional cultures
that developed historically and analyzes how the cultural history shapes the
Southeast Asian region's current culture. The book is written in a lively and
interesting style, and contains the Southeast Asian region's languages, foods, music/
dance, art/literature, religions, holidays, lifestyle, and most importantly contemporary
culture in the country today"— Provided by publisher.
  ISBN 978-1-61228-565-8 (library bound)
  1. Southeast Asia—Civilization—Juvenile literature. 2. Southeast Asia--Social life
and customs—Juvenile literature. I. Title.
  DS625.N325 2014
  959--dc23

                                                              2014013223

eBook ISBN: 9781612286044

PUBLISHER'S NOTE: This story is based on the author's extensive research, which he believes to be accurate. Documentation of this research is on pages 59–61.

The Internet sites referenced herein were active as of the publication date. Due to the fleeting nature of some web sites, we cannot guarantee they will all be active when you are reading this book.

To reflect current usage, we have chosen to use the secular era designations BCE ("before the common era") and CE ("of the common era") instead of the traditional designations BC ("before Christ") and AD (*anno Domini,* "in the year of the Lord").

CONTENTS

INTRODUCTION
A Region of Diversity and Dangers

"I heard several sounds like thunder," a forty-two-year-old woman named Mukinem said. "I was so scared I was shaking."[1] Mukinem and her family are among the thousands of people who live near Mount Merapi, a large volcano on Indonesia's southern island of Java. In October 2010, the peak exploded in fiery fury, causing widespread ruin. Eruptions continued for over a month. A news cameraman who reported on the eruptions was in awe. "Several houses and cattle have been burned by the hot cloud from the mountain," he said. "All the houses are blanketed in ash, completely white. The leaves have been burned off the trees."[2]

Merapi is only one of seventy-six historically active volcanoes in Indonesia,[3] a land made up of many islands. The southernmost nation in the region of Southeast Asia, it is the most volcanic country on Earth. More than 1,000 miles (1,600 kilometers) northeast of Java lies the Philippines. Another Southeast Asian nation composed of numerous islands, the Philippines has more than twenty active volcanoes.

But Southeast Asia is a region of stark extremes. Despite the area's highly active volcanoes, for example, all of its countries are blessed with striking natural beauty. This includes countless scenic mountains, most of them covered by lush blue-green forests. They overlook vast expanses of calm, sunlit sea. Yet among those peaks, volcanic dangers occasionally lurk.

Almost Wiped from the Map

Southeast Asia's overall climate is part of another of the region's sets of extremes, or tradeoffs. On the positive side of this tradeoff, all of its countries enjoy warm, pleasant weather nearly year round. Typical is still another island nation—Malaysia, situated just north of Indonesia. No less warm is the tiny country of Singapore, perched on Malaysia's southernmost tip.

There is a distinctly dangerous aspect of this climatic tradeoff, however. The warmth that bathes the land portions of these island nations also heats up the nearby shallow seas. And those warm waters sometimes fuel and intensify big storms called typhoons. About nineteen of them form near the Philippines each year, and on average, eight or nine make landfall.[4] Some three hundred thousand people died when the Haiphong Typhoon smashed into Southeast Asia in 1881.

More recently, in November 2013, Typhoon Haiyan struck. One of the strongest ocean storms ever recorded, it killed more than six thousand people in the Philippines. Stormchaser Josh Morgerman recalled that Tacloban City was almost wiped from the map. It became "a horrid landscape of smashed buildings and completely defoliated trees," he said.[5]

The Ravages of Deforestation

Deadly Haiyan claimed lives in Vietnam, too. That long, thin nation lies on the eastern side of the big peninsula that juts out of Asia's southeastern corner. Malaysia's western portion occupies the peninsula's southernmost section. Directly north of it, and west of Vietnam, stretch Cambodia, Thailand, Laos, and Myanmar (formerly Burma).

Along with Southeast Asia's island nations, those on the peninsula feature a hugely diverse collection of plants and animals. Most of them exist in these countries' dense rainforests. Together with some in Africa and South America, they are among the world's few remaining rainforests.

Moreover, these magnificent, life-giving jungles may soon be gone. They are disappearing at an alarming rate, as deforestation ravages the entire region. The Philippines is one of the worst offenders. According to the Filipino environmental group Kalikasan, "The Philippines is among countries with the fastest loss of forest cover around the world. It ranks fourth among the world's top ten most threatened forest hotspots."[6]

As the forests vanish, so do many of the animal and plant species that depend on them. This means that the countries of Southeast Asia are changing at an amazingly quick pace. The forests and the life forms within them are part of these nations' identities. And a growing number of the region's inhabitants are fighting hard to slow the rate of deforestation. They hope this will preserve some of their splendid natural diversity for future generations.

Proboscis monkey

7

CHAPTER ONE
An Unforgettable Shared Experience

"I was resting on the bed," recalled Asian-American journalist Brenda Paik Sunoo. On that day, December 26, 2004, she was staying at a hotel on the coast of Thailand. Suddenly, a hotel worker "came running to our bungalow screaming, 'Look! Look!'" Sunoo hurried to her balcony. There, she was shocked to see a churning wall of water "crashing on the shore." As she watched in terror, "tons of moving water swept away everything in its path."[1]

The frightening wave Sunoo witnessed was part of the most destructive tsunami, or huge sea wave, in recent human memory. It struck the coasts of Indonesia, Thailand, and other Southeast Asian nations on that fateful December day. Millions of people across the region found themselves fighting for their lives.

One of them was a British man, Aaron Le Boutillier. He was working on the Thai island of Koh Phi Phi when the monster wave arrived. Although he was, in his words, "badly cut up," he managed to survive. But many others around him were not so fortunate. The day after the disaster, while searching for missing friends, "nothing could prepare me for what I was about to see," he later remembered. "In total, there were about six hundred bodies," including "babies, toddlers, children, adolescents, and adults."[2]

Massive Aid Efforts

The historic 2004 tsunami devastated many of Southeast Asia's coastal regions, causing widespread death and destruction. Yet afterward numerous residents remarked on one positive aspect of the calamity. Namely, it brought together millions of people from separate nations with different backgrounds, languages, and religions. For a few terrible days, they shared an unforgettable experience. More importantly, they showed that in an emergency they can work together for the region's greater good.

In Phuket, Thailand, a third wave from the 2004 tsunami hits the Chedi Hotel's restaurant.

First, the Southeast Asian countries least affected by the disaster immediately helped those worst hit. To its credit, the smallest nation in the region, Singapore, stepped up and delivered massive aid to its suffering neighbors. It sent them more than one thousand military and other experts. They helped to organize searches for survivors, as well as cleanup efforts. A majority of the personnel went to northwestern Indonesia, where the wave damage was particularly bad. Singapore also sent many ships and helicopters carrying doctors, nurses, and medical supplies. Other ships brought backhoes and other heavy equipment to clear debris from streets and airport runways.

Meanwhile, Malaysia wasted no time in sending enormous amounts of aid to the region's harder-hit countries. It did this despite the fact that almost seventy Malaysians lost their lives to the tsunami. The Malaysian government sent rescue teams to Indonesia to look for survivors. The humanitarian group Mercy Malaysia also dispatched large groups of doctors and nurses and massive amounts of food and clothing for homeless victims.

Even individual Malaysian businesses pitched in. A representative for Pelangi Beach & Spa Resort announced that it had been "spared from major devastation," and that the hotel's management wanted to help "the less fortunate ones" affected by the disaster. To that end, they created a crisis fund. "Every single dollar contributed towards the fund," the representative told the press, "will be channeled to the victims who had lost their loved ones as well as homes."[3]

Return of the Tribal Network?

Just as important as the search teams, doctors, and other physical aid was providing the affected areas with vital information. The waves had knocked out numerous communication networks. As a result, families and friends often did not know if their loved ones in the hardest-hit areas were alive or dead. So right after the tsunami, many local residents who did have internet access started up blogs. The bloggers began collecting important information about the disaster-related situations in their communities and posting it online.

Moreover, many of those blogs remained active in the months and years that followed. By 2005, there were some fifteen thousand of them in Malaysia alone.[4] Online visitors talked about the tsunami and other disasters, bringing the peoples and cultures of the region closer together. Before telephones, radio, and television existed, Malaysian blogger Jack Tuan commented, people communicated through a "tribal word-of-mouth network." He thinks that "blogs are a natural extension of that."[5]

Most of all, though, Tuan and the other bloggers believe their efforts will make future natural disasters in the region less painful. One of their number, Malaysian Ashwar Abd Aziz, recalls an example of how a blog post helped in the wake of the 2004 tragedy. On the day following the tsunami, Aziz says, his father asked if he would use the computer to contact his friends, members of 4x4 off-road clubs. "He asked me whether [those] friends could gather used clothing, books," and "second-hand school shoes to be donated to the victims." Aziz complied and soon after, club members and blog readers from far and wide used their off-road vehicles to deliver supplies to survivors in need.[6]

When the 2004 tsunami struck southern Thailand, the small island of Koh Phi Phi suffered awful devastation. Nearly a week after the tsunami, work to clear the debris and repair the damage had only just begun.

Even more impressive was the formation of a central clearing house for thousands of scattered bloggers. Its official name is the Southeast Asia Earthquake and Tsunami Blog. But most people call it the "SEA-EAT Blog" for short. People from across the region and around the globe reached out to one another through the blog, providing information and offering help.

In these ways, a horrible tragedy ended up having a positive and lasting effect on Southeast Asia. It brought large numbers of Indonesians, Malaysians, Thais, Vietnamese, and others together. It made them realize they are neighbors with common needs and hopes that far outweigh any of their differences.

Many people died in the Indonesian town of Banda Aceh during the 2004 tsunami. Here, in 2008, some of the surviving citizens take part in a tsunami drill designed to better prepare the residents for any future tsunamis.

When People Work Together

Southeast Asian bloggers played an unexpected and major role in the relief efforts after the 2004 tsunami. These volunteers used their websites to bring together people from across the region. Through the central SEA-EAT blog, they gave untold numbers of Southeast Asians a way to both help and learn about one another. A native of the Asian country of Sri Lanka now living in the United States posted the following message on SEA-EAT. In it she tells how SEA-EAT and its bloggers build unity and friendship among the peoples of numerous Asian nations. The blog, she says,

> is a shining example of how everyday people *can* make a *huge* difference when they work together. You will never know the full ripple effect of your efforts—the money that was raised, the posting that motivated someone to start a project, to volunteer, to donate, the people you helped reunite, the child whose school was rebuilt because someone saw a posting here. I have to tell you it motivated me with [my own web]site. So continue the good work. Post the appeals, the news, the situation reports. Our best role as virtual relief workers, I think, is to build bridges between needs and wants, and that is exactly what you are doing.[7]

A group of Southeast Asian women sort through bags and boxes of clothes and other items donated by people around the world after the deadly 2004 tsunami disaster.

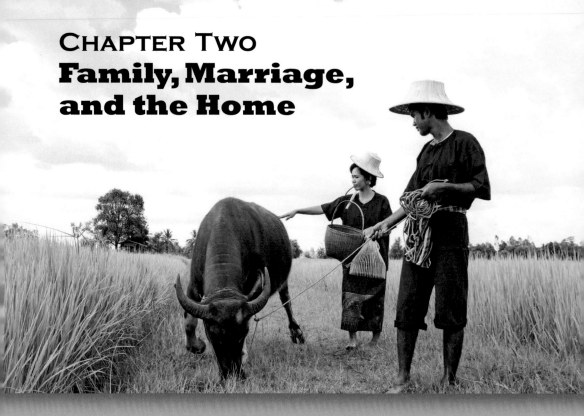

CHAPTER TWO
Family, Marriage, and the Home

"I am who I am because of my family; their success is my success, and my shame is their shame."[1] So goes an old Filipino saying. It dates back countless generations to that nation's pre-modern culture, in which farming was the main means of making a living. Practically every couple had children. And all members of a family had to contribute their share of work to ensure the household's survival. Such was the case not only in the Philippines, but all across Southeast Asia in those days.

Moreover, this custom did not change much after modern nations arose in the region in the 1900s. The family continued to be society's core unit, and parents still felt it was their primary duty to have and care for children. Born in Vietnam in the 1960s, Dan The Le remembers how his parents felt about their duties. "I guess all parents back then," he says, lacked the "option to be anything" else except for good parents. They felt like it was their job "just to follow the rule" of society and "take care of [the] family."[2]

Family Feelings and Duties

Even today, the Southeast Asian family remains tight-knit, with all members feeling responsibility toward one another. "My family [has] a lot of respect and love," Dan explains. In large part, he thinks, it is because "we share the same roots."[3]

With so much stress placed on family duties, children traditionally lived in the family home right up until they were married. Even today, elderly parents and grandparents are never allowed to live alone. They always have at least one relative to help and support them in their old age. By tradition, therefore, if times are hard for a family, a young person is often expected to sacrifice. It is not unusual for him or her to give up plans for an education and get a job to help the family make ends meet.

In Southeast Asia, family is very important. Younger generations have a responsibility to take care of older family members as they age.

It is not surprising that in such highly devoted families the parents enjoy a great deal of respect. People in positions of authority, like teachers and government officials, are viewed much like parental figures and given considerable respect. In Indonesia, for example, *bapak* (bah-PAHK) is the word not only for father, but also for any respected man in society (similar to "sir"). Therefore, people see it as rude to argue with social "superiors."

Household Gender Roles

There has rarely been any question about who is superior in the average household. Although Southeast Asians show both their parents a lot of respect, traditionally more of it goes to the father than to the mother. This is because, with few exceptions, the region's societies are patriarchal—families are led by men. Thus, the husband/father is the head of the household and makes most major family decisions. Also, he and his wife usually settle in the area where *his* relatives, rather than hers, live.

The wife/mother is still important within the family, however. She is viewed as the chief caregiver and her primary roles are to raise the children, cook, and clean. And while men may help with family duties, it's usually not considered their place to do so. Alex Thai Nguyen is another native of Vietnam who was born in the 1960s. He says that in his country, "women are more known to be in the kitchen," than men are.[4]

Many modern Vietnamese and Southeast Asians would view Alex's remark about women in the kitchen as a bit old-fashioned. While traditional family roles still play a large part in the cultures of these nations, these roles are rapidly changing. As television and the Internet expose people to Western lifestyles, more young women in Singapore, Malaysia, Vietnam, and other countries are delaying marriage and childbirth in order to pursue careers. Today, these women are increasingly seen performing jobs that were previously reserved for men, and are even running their own businesses.

Southeast Asian women are usually responsible for household duties like cooking. Here, a young mother in Myanmar prepares lunch as her children play.

This family photo from a modern Southeast Asian wedding shows how formal, elaborate, and colorful these celebrations are. Note that the bride wears a Western-style white wedding dress.

Getting Married

Another crucial family and social custom is steadily changing across Southeast Asia. It is the manner in which men and women get married in the first place. In past generations, the tradition was for marriages to be arranged by parents, relatives, or matchmakers. The bride and groom had little say in the matter. And they were only rarely in love with each other. Even when he was growing up in the 1960s and 1970s, Dan The Le says, marriage was usually "all about arrangement." So most young couples did not have "a love relationship."[5]

Today arranged marriages still exist in the region, especially in small villages in the countryside. But most Southeast Asian young people choose their spouse. Despite this, it is uncommon for a man or woman to marry without their family's approval. No matter what the motivation for people to get married, weddings are major events for families and even entire communities.

Southeast Asian wedding ceremonies and receptions vary in their details from country to country. They also vary from religion to religion. There are Hindu, Muslim, Buddhist, and Christian versions, to name only a few. Yet all have basic similarities. Typically these wedding celebrations feature elaborate and colorful costumes and decorations, huge spreads of traditional food dishes, and much music, dancing, and gift-giving.

A Mixture of Old and New

In recent times it has become common to mix certain Western wedding customs with local ones. In such weddings, brides may forgo traditional colorful gowns or costumes in favor of the white wedding dress that is common in the West. Still, many Southeast Asian weddings continue to feature the formal costumes and customs passed down through dozens of generations. As with family customs and gender roles, it is common throughout the region to see a mixture of both old and new. In Singapore, for example, many brides of Chinese heritage wear a white wedding dress during the day, and then switch to the more traditional red *qun kua* (embroidered skirt and jacket) for the afternoon or evening festivities.

This cluster of longhouses is located in Malaysia. The dwellings rest on stilts so that incoming floodwaters will pass beneath them.

Traditional and Modern Houses

By tradition, when Southeast Asian couples marry they set up new households in which to raise their children. Today, it is common across the region to see many family homes that are as modern-looking as those in Western countries. Some of the Southeast Asian versions are single-family houses in the countryside or suburbs. Others are apartments in high-rise buildings in the cities. Most of those constructed in recent years have electricity, running water, flush toilets, and television sets. Yet houses built in the region's more traditional styles remain a common sight. Most of those located in coastal areas or lands prone to flooding are erected on stilts. These poles are most often from about 4 to 8 feet

(1.2 to 2.4 meters) tall. They allow big waves and flood waters caused by storms to pass under the house, sparing the structure from serious damage. Such houses were originally made almost entirely of plant matter, including wood, bamboo, and palm leaves. Modern raised houses are more frequently built from brick or concrete. One type of traditional raised home is the longhouse. Some of these homes have a single communal space, as well as private units for each family. Others consist of large spaces which are used by the entire community of five, ten, or more families. Longhouses are particularly common in Vietnam and on the large island of Borneo.

CHAPTER THREE
A Fantastic Mix of Faiths and Beliefs

A German man named Jochen Schlingmann loves to travel. He recorded over twenty years of his Southeast Asian travel experiences in a blog he calls *Asienreisender*. Fittingly, it means "Asia traveler" in German. When Schlingmann first arrived in Southeast Asia, the number and diversity of the area's belief systems astounded him. "There are really a lot of different religions here," he wrote. It is "not only the major world religions alone," he added. Those faiths also "split up into many particular sub-religions."[1]

The world religions Schlingmann refers to are Buddhism, Islam, and Christianity, and to a lesser extent Hinduism. Most Southeast Asians belong to one or another of these faiths. For example, about 93 percent of Filipinos are Christians. In Thailand, by contrast, 95 percent of the residents are Buddhists. That faith is slightly more prevalent in Cambodia, where over 96 percent of the people follow it.

Meanwhile, in Indonesia some 86 percent of the inhabitants are Muslims, followers of Islam. Malaysia also has many Muslims, who make up 60 percent of the populace. But its breakdown of beliefs is more mixed. Almost 20 percent of Malaysians are Buddhists, 9 percent are Christians, and about 6 percent are Hindus.

Buddhist Beliefs and Activities

Buddhism first began in India in either the fifth or sixth century BCE, more than two thousand years ago. A young prince named Siddhartha Gautama was disturbed by the widespread human suffering he witnessed. Over time, Buddhists believe, he came to realize a great truth. It was that human suffering comes from attachments, or desires for things like material goods and freedom from death, and from ignorance, or not seeing the world as it really is. Thereafter, people called him the Buddha, meaning "enlightened one."

The Buddha also said that people can overcome suffering by following eight positive principles. Buddhists call them the Eightfold Path. The first of the eight, the late Buddhist monk Ajaan Lee Dhammadharo wrote, is Right View, or "seeing in line with the truth." There are also Right Resolve, or "thinking in ways that will lead to well-being," and Right Speech, "speaking in line with the truth."[2]

The Buddha's followers told others about these and other constructive aspects of the Eightfold Path. Many found them appealing, and Buddhism rapidly expanded. It spread to Burma and China and from there into Thailand and other sections of Southeast Asia. There Buddhists built shrines and temples, many of which still exist.

In those and newer temples, modern Buddhist monks conduct colorful ceremonies on the faith's holidays. One of the biggest festivals is Wesak (VESS-ak), held during the full moon in May. It celebrates the Buddha's birthday. Buddhists also visit the shrines and temples whenever they feel the urge. Typically they meditate, or sit quietly and focus their thoughts. By doing this, they hope to calm their minds, and increase awareness and control of their own thoughts.

...dhist monks meditate at a ...ple in Laos. They are not ...rshiping the statue of the ...ddha they face, as he ...s not a god. Rather, ...is revered as a wise ...rson who discovered ...portant truths about ...e human condition.

Worshiping in Mosques

In Indonesia, Malaysia, and Brunei, Islam is the main faith. About 218 million Muslims live in Indonesia alone (as of 2014).[3] Adding them to the Muslims in other Southeast Asian nations reveals that Islam is the region's predominate faith. In fact, says Singapore-based scholar Parag Khanna, "there are more Muslims in Southeast Asia than there are in the entire Arab world."[4]

Like Muslims everywhere, those in Indonesia and other Southeast Asian nations revere the same god that Jews and Christians do. But for Muslims, the way they worship God, whom Muslims call Allah, is slightly different. Tahmena Bokhari, a social worker who spent time with and studied the region's Muslim communities, explains that Islam began in Arabia in the 600s CE. The angel Gabriel visited a local merchant named Muhammad. Gabriel said the man was Allah's final prophet, or messenger to other people. The angel also dictated to Muhammad the text of Islam's holy book, the Quran (or Qur'an, or Koran).

The main principles of the new faith became known as the Five Pillars. In Bokhari's words, one is the "declaration of faith" that there is no god except Allah, and that Muhammad is Allah's messenger. Two others are "prayer five times per day" and "fasting during the month of Ramadan," the ninth month of the Islamic calendar. Muslims also must give "charity to the poor." Finally, they are expected to perform the "Hajj," a journey to Muhammad's hometown of Mecca, at least "once in a lifetime."[5]

The chants of muezzins (myoo-EZ-inz) are a common sound across the Islamic regions of Southeast Asia. They are the religious officials who call the region's Muslims to prayer five times each day. When possible, the faithful gather to pray in mosques, their community places of worship. Before kneeling for prayer, worshipers normally wash their faces, hands, arms, and feet. Also, both men and women cover their heads out of respect for Allah.

Supernatural Beliefs

Numerous other belief systems exist in Southeast Asia. Some, best described as traditional folk beliefs, are common in villages in the

In 2013, hundreds of Muslim worshipers gather at the Istiglal Mosque in Jakarta, Indonesia, during the holy month of Ramadan.

countryside. Christians, Muslims, and Buddhists throughout Southeast Asia have also retained many of their traditional beliefs. These newer religions usually did not replace old beliefs; instead they added to them. Large numbers of Southeast Asians believe that amulets or charms can ward off spells or the evil eye. While about half of Muslims in the region believe in spirits and witchcraft, they are the least likely group to use talismans. This is because the Quran instructs Muslims not to rely on objects for protection, but instead to seek protection from Allah.[6]

Another folk belief widely accepted in the region deals with another kind of spirit—that of one's ancestor. Ancestor worship holds that the spirits of deceased relatives can visit the living. So believers sometimes show respect to those spirits by praying to them. They may even have a family altar in their home where the ancestors are invited to visit. Families may burn incense or candles at these altars, and offer small gifts or food.

A large number of Southeast Asians accept the existence of still other sorts of spirits. Spirits can be good or evil, and even objects can contain spirits or energy. To protect themselves, people may make offerings to the spirits to keep them happy. The Hungry Ghost festival is celebrated each summer in Singapore, Malaysia, and Vietnam. It is believed that ghosts wander the earth on this day each year. They must be fed, paid money, and entertained in order to keep them from creating chaos for the living.

People sometimes enlist the services of spiritual healers or masters to protect themselves from spirits or spells. Malaysians call such a person a *bomoh* (BOH-moh), while the Thai word for him is *maw pii*. The residents of southern Indonesia call a spiritual master a *dukun* (DOO-koon).

Residents of Singapore lay out fruit and other foods in an effort to appease ghosts that are thought to roam the earth for one day each summer.

Cao Dai and Other Vietnamese Faiths

Among Southeast Asia's nations, Vietnam is, religiously speaking, the most unusual. First, it is very difficult to know who believes what there. In large part this is because of the outcome of the Vietnam War. After the United States withdrew in 1973, communist North Vietnam absorbed democratic South Vietnam, creating a single country. The communist government is officially non-religious. And its population is reported as about 82 percent atheist, 10 percent Buddhist, and 7 percent Christian. However, most outside experts suspect that more Vietnamese are religious than the government admits. Actual percentages for various faiths are unknown. But it is estimated that at least a few million of the residents belong to a religion called Cao Dai (kow dye). Established in 1926, it combines elements of Buddhism, Christianity, Taoism, and other faiths. Cao Dai teaches that all human religions contain certain truths, and come from the same source—God. Believers also hold that all people are brothers and sisters who should love and respect one another. The revered saints of Cao Dai include Jesus, Muhammad, Moses, Roman general Julius Caesar, and noted French novelist Victor Hugo.

Pictured is a Cao Dai temple in Vietnam. The Cao Dai faith holds that all religions are equal in worth, in part because each contains certain truths originally set down by God.

CHAPTER FOUR
Vanishing Animals and Rainforests

Alam the orangutan was just a little baby when a poacher killed his mother and kidnapped him. Each year poachers, criminals who steal or kill wild animals, take many young orangutans from their families. They then sell them to people who want to keep the creatures as pets. Having pet orangutans is illegal in Southeast Asia.

Alam turned out to be lucky. In May 2013, when he was eighteen months old, members of Sumatra's Orangutan Information Center (OIC) rescued him. They forced the farmer who had bought him from the poacher to hand him over.

OIC's founder, Panut Hadisiswoyo, tells about Alam's habitat, or home area. "It is certain," he says, "that Alam's mother would have been killed." That would make it easier "for the poacher to capture him for the pet trade." Hadisiswoyo thinks that the baby came "from an area of forest that is being cleared for development." It may have been "for oil palm plantations or roads."[1]

Soon to Be Gone Forever?

The OIC, which is dedicated to helping wild orangutans, hopes to eventually release Alam back into the wild. In the meantime, most of his fellow orangutans are in deep trouble. They are members of an endangered species, or one threatened with extinction. In 1900, hundreds of thousands of orangutans lived in Southeast Asia. The World Wildlife Fund (WWF) estimates that the orangutan population on the Indonesian island of Sumatra is currently around seven thousand. And it is shrinking fast.

This Indonesian orangutan and its baby are endangered. Orangutans spend most of their lives in the treetops of rainforests, which are disappearing rapidly across much of Southeast Asia.

It is not only the illegal pet trade that threatens them. Some Indonesians like to eat orangutans, which has created another market for poachers. Most of all, however, these noble creatures are in danger because their habitats are rapidly disappearing. "The forests are under huge pressure here in Sumatra," Hadisiswoyo states. Sadly, the orangutans "are losing their habitat at an alarming rate." That makes it "easier for poachers to get hold of protected and endangered wildlife."[2]

The threatened "wildlife" Hadisiswoyo speaks of includes far more than just orangutans. Another species presently in trouble in Indonesia is the single-horned Javan rhinoceros. The last few surviving specimens live in a national park on the country's large island of Java. A large reptile, the Komodo dragon, is also endangered. So are the local tigers, gibbons, shrews, and numerous others.

This Asian rhinoceros is called the Javan rhino or the lesser one-horned rhino. As of 2014, it was so close to the brink of extinction that no more than fifty individuals were left.

A Komodo dragon exposes its lengthy tongue. Another endangered species in Southeast Asia, the dragon lives by hunting birds, insects, and mammals up to the size of a goat!

What's more, the loss of animal habitats due to deforestation is not confined to Indonesia. Once plentiful animal species are disappearing all over Southeast Asia. Like their Indonesian cousins, the last few orangutans in Malaysia are seriously endangered. Other creatures that may soon become extinct in Malaysia are its tigers, elephants, rhinos, and four of its turtle species.

Similarly, the Philippines may soon lose the dwarf buffalo. Also on the verge of extinction in that country are the warty pig, forest frog, and giant golden-crowned flying fox. Hundreds of miles to the west, meanwhile, Cambodia is in the same dilemma. There, dolphins, elephants, tigers, green peafowl, and many others may soon be gone forever.

Elephants roam through Gunung Leuser National Park on the Indonesian island of Sumatra. They are in danger of extinction thanks to forest loss caused by the expansion of human civilization.

Causes of Forest Loss

The massive deforestation that is destroying these animals' homes has a number of causes. One is swiftly expanding human settlements. Year after year in Cambodia, the Philippines, Malaysia, Indonesia, and elsewhere in Southeast Asia, towns and cities grow larger. Several of the cities have become badly overcrowded. So thousands of people move to the countryside each year. They cut down large expanses of rainforest to make way for roads, housing developments, and shopping malls.

Even more destructive are the activities of numerous big companies that want to exploit the rainforests for profit. Particularly destructive are logging companies, which remove millions of trees each year. The environmental group WWF-Malaysia adds that "illegal removal of forest products" is also a problem. "Malaysia's land surface was once almost entirely covered with forest," the

A waterfall in Thailand overlooks an agricultural plantation. Local forests are regularly cleared to make way for such large-scale farms. Also, more and more housing developments sit on land that was once covered by rainforest.

In Sarawak, Malaysia, a large stretch of rainforest has been recently cleared using the slash-and-burn method, which involves cutting and then burning the trees and plants. Farmers will later grow their crops in the fertile soil that has been created by the ashes of the nutrient-rich plants.

group's website explains. But today the forests cover less than 60 percent of the country. Between 1983 and 2003 alone, a forested area "about four times the size of Singapore" was lost.[3]

The same problem plagues the Philippines. Before the start of the twentieth century, ancient rainforests covered some 70 percent of that country's land masses. Then, states the Filipino environmental group Kalikasan, "Large scale, export oriented commercial logging was introduced by the American colonizers."[4] That industry grew at an astonishingly quick pace. And by the late 1900s around 4 square miles (10 square kilometers) of forest disappeared each and every day. As a result, in 2014 only about 3 percent of the country's original rainforests were left.[5]

Failure Not an Option

A growing number of citizens in the Southeast Asian countries are deeply concerned about these environmental problems. They want to save the region's remaining rainforests. Those forests, they say, are more than habitats for large numbers of animal species. They also help to regulate the flow of life-giving water into streams, rivers, and reservoirs. In addition, the rainforests supply numerous plants from which thousands of human medicines are made.

Indeed, huge numbers of people depend on the rainforests to live, says Cambodian environmental activist Eoun Sopapheap. "If we lose those trees, we lose everything." To reverse the damage already done, he declares, is "up to us."[6] For their own part, Sopapheap and his fellow Cambodian activists track down and report on illegal logging operations. Meanwhile, both private activists and government officials in other Southeast Asian nations are employing other approaches.

Together, these programs have made some progress. The fact that little Alam and several other orangutans have been saved is proof of that. Yet a great deal remains to be done to halt the continuing losses. And those involved in these efforts know it well. "Correct decisions must be made and implemented immediately," Kalikasan cautions. "Time is running out," and "failure is no longer an option."[7]

Forest-Saving Efforts

Eoun Sopapheap and his fellow Cambodian activists regularly seek out illegal loggers in their country's rainforests. One day in 2012,[8] the searchers heard the sound of a chainsaw in the distance. Soon they found a man unlawfully cutting down a tree. The logger told them he knew what he was doing was wrong. But he was poor and needed the money to support his family. After taking away the chainsaw, Sopapheap and the others let him go. They were more interested in finding his boss, the leader of the illegal logging outfit, who they hoped would end up in jail.

A few hundred miles to the southeast, meanwhile, the governments of the Philippines and Malaysia were taking a different approach. In

1996, they signed an agreement which created the Turtle Islands Heritage Protected Area. The Turtle Islands lie on both sides of the border between the two nations. The ongoing program protects the wildlife and their habitats on the islands. Thousands of turtles nest on the islands every year. It's the only major turtle nesting ground in the area, and one of only ten remaining nesting grounds in the world.

Still another effort to save the forests is managed by the World Wildlife Fund. Beginning in the 1960s, it installed branches across Southeast Asia. In 1991, the group worked with the Indonesian government to create the Indonesian National Biodiversity Action Plan. The plan expanded that country's national parks and protected endangered animals.

A logger uses a chainsaw to clear a tree from a rainforest in the Philippines. Although that country's forests are shrinking, some substantial sections remain on the islands of Bohol, Palawa, and Mindanao.

Common Foods and Dining Customs

Many foreign visitors to Southeast Asia have commented on a particular phrase they had often heard there. Locals across the region frequently greet one another by asking, "Have you eaten your rice today?"[1] In reality, they are not inquiring about rice-eating. Rice is by far the most commonly eaten food in the Southeast Asian countries. And socially speaking, it stands for prosperity and well-being.

So the phrase actually means something like, "How is it going?" or "How is life treating you?"

Local Versus Regional Foods

A sort of universal food in the region, rice is a part of most of the local meals. Yet the way it is prepared and served often differs considerably from one area to another. First, people tend to pair it with whatever vegetables and/or meats are most common or popular in their area. Also, locals sometimes like to cook rice and other common foods in certain traditional ways.

For example, noted Vietnamese chef Luke Nguyen tells a charming story about a trip he took to neighboring Thailand. He wanted to sample a cooking style popular among the Hmong people. Living in parts of Vietnam, Thailand, and Laos, the Hmong are known for cooking some of their foods in cut bamboo stalks. They say that the bamboo gives the food an herb-like, earthy flavor.

A Hmong cook named Yoda had "promised to show me his favorite local pork dish," Nguyen recalls, which he "cooked in bamboo." On arriving in Yoda's village, Nguyen was in for a surprise. Namely he was expected to cut his own bamboo for the dish. "I had to chop down a tall bamboo tree with only a small blunt machete!" the traveler says. "It was taking so long that I was expecting Yoda to say, 'Use the force, Luke!'"[2]

In spite of such local cooking styles, pork and rice are among certain foods eaten across all or most of Southeast Asia. Various kinds of fish are also in that category. This is because most of the region's nations have extensive coastlines that border the sea. In fact, fish is the primary source of protein in Southeast Asia. Other

Eaten with many meals in Southeast Asia, rice is one of the region's most important staple foods.

This seafood soup from Thailand is only one of the numerous Southeast Asian dishes that use ingredients from the region's Indian and Pacific Oceans.

popular meats include not only pork, but also beef, chicken, lamb, deer, and lizard. Meats are most often cut into small pieces before cooking.

Fruits, Vegetables, and Spices

Because tropical fruits grow all across Southeast Asia, they constitute another kind of universal food in the region. Among the most common fruits eaten are coconuts, pineapples, papayas, bananas, and star fruit. Another popular fruit, the durian, has a hard, spiky skin, but the center is soft and tasty.

Vegetables consumed almost everywhere in the region include eggplant, spinach, lettuce, bean sprouts, and scallions. Also popular are sweet potato greens, corn, luffa (a cucumber-like plant), bamboo shoots, mushrooms, lemongrass, and daikon (a white radish). In addition, Southeast Asians eat the leaves of numerous green plants. One of the more common is the pandan, which features fan-shaped groups of long leaves. Pandan leaves have a "sweet fragrance and color," says Malaysian-born housewife Kiran Tarun. They are used in many "savory recipes" throughout Southeast Asia, she explains. "Fresh pandan leaves are torn into strips or tied in knots to infuse a distinct floral aroma and flavor."[3]

Many Southeast Asians like eating at least some of their vegetables raw. When cooked, vegetables, like meats, are most often cut up into bite-sized pieces first. Vegetable dishes, along with dishes that mix vegetables with meats, are generally fried in a wok, steamed, or boiled.

These foods do not occupy the wok by themselves, however. Southeast Asian cooking is widely known for its numerous bursts of flavor provided by a wide array of tasty spices. In fact, spices were among the primary goods that drew European traders to the region in the late medieval centuries. In Indonesia and elsewhere, they found ginger, garlic, cinnamon, nutmeg, cloves, and several others.

Also widespread in Southeast Asia are palm trees, which yield sugar for sweetening foods. During his Cambodian trip, Luke Nguyen saw native workers making the sugar in the same manner it has been made for centuries in the region. "Skilled climbers scale palm trees," he says. Then they "wedge the palm nuts between two sticks and extract the sweet juice from the nut. This juice is slowly cooked in large woks over low heat." Finally it becomes "a thick, sweet, golden syrup," and they extract the sugar from the syrup.[4]

Polite Eating Habits

Most foreign visitors to Southeast Asia remark not only about the delicious native food dishes, but also about local dining customs. Many restaurants in the cities serve food the same way American and other Western ones do. The same is true of some Southeast Asian homes. However, a number of restaurants and many homes still feature dining customs more traditional to the region.

For example, the time-honored way of serving is to place all of the food dishes before the diners at the same time. They then pick

A cook in Singapore's Chinese district fries pastries in a large wok. Woks of all sizes are used in kitchens across Southeast Asia.

and choose what they want a little at a time. Food is eaten with chopsticks, the fingers of the right hand, or Western flatware.

Several dining customs in the region are based on local religious beliefs. Muslims do not eat and should not be served pork, for instance. Similarly, Hindus refrain from consuming beef. And some Buddhists do not eat any animal products, including dairy like butter and cheese. Smart travelers try to learn the accepted, polite eating habits before arriving in Southeast Asia. That way the locals are less likely to view them as ill-mannered.

This mouth-watering spread of traditional Vietnamese dishes features numerous kinds of vegetables prepared in various ways.

The durian, shown here in its natural state, is often called the "king of fruits" by Southeast Asians. It grows all across the region.

The King of Fruits

The durian is so popular across Southeast Asia that people there call it the king of fruits. Yet it is also the subject of many disagreements, especially among outsiders who have never encountered it before. This is because the durian tastes much different than it smells. A number of natives say they like its odor. But many others, including most European visitors, think it smells awful. Some have gone so far as to compare it to rotting garbage. Back in the 1800s, the famous British scientist Alfred Russel Wallace paid a long visit to Southeast Asia. He tried the durian and liked it, but did mention its smell. "The durian is generally mentioned as a fruit much liked by natives," he later wrote. But its "offensive smell renders it disagreeable to Europeans." Wallace noted that the fruit is oval-shaped and has a rough, thorny skin. Beneath that skin, he said, rests a soft, yellowish, and tasty pulp. "This pulp is the eatable part," he explained. He went on to describe the taste, saying it is like "a rich custard highly flavoured with almonds."[5] As was the case in Wallace's time, today the durian is found throughout Southeast Asia. But the biggest growers and exporters are Thailand, Malaysia, and Indonesia.

A durian has been sliced in order to show its yellowish pulp, which most Southeast Asians love.

CHAPTER SIX
Sports and Other Leisure Activities

"I'm lost for words to describe how sad we are. It's heartbreaking."[1] Phone Myint Khaing, a young resident of Myanmar, spoke these words on December 17, 2013. He was terribly upset that his country's national football team had just lost an important match. The opposing team, from Indonesia, had won by a single goal. That had knocked Myanmar out of the running to win the Southeast Asian Games. Myanmar's fans were so upset that many of them rioted in the stadium.

The Region's Favorite Sport

Such passionate reactions to losing or winning football matches are common in Southeast Asia. This is because football is overall the favorite sport throughout the region. By "football," the Indonesians, Filipinos, Thais, Malaysians, and other natives do not mean the American game of that name. As in most other parts of the world, football in Southeast Asia is what Americans call soccer.

Most Southeast Asian children—girls as well as boys—play the game in backyards and fields from a young age. They also play on their school teams. Meanwhile, people of all ages avidly watch their national teams play on TV. In addition, they follow the sport on the Internet, sometimes reading blogs written by other football lovers.

One of those blogs is written by Vietnamese fan Erick Bui. "I have a lot of friends overseas who are also football fans," he writes. "They often question me about Vietnamese football." He says this is because it's hard to find much information about Southeast Asian football outside the region. A football blog written in English, Bui thinks, "can be an essential link between Vietnam and the world. I have the passion and decent football knowledge, so I really enjoy blogging about Vietnamese football."[2]

Water Sports and Martial Arts

A number of other athletic pursuits are popular in Southeast Asia, several of which are water sports. This is not surprising considering the region's geography. Most of its nations have long ocean coastlines with huge numbers of bays, inlets, and sandy beaches.

An Indonesian boy surfs at one of his nation's thousands of sandy beaches. Water sports are widely popular in Southeast Asia.

As a result, both the natives and foreign tourists regularly enjoy fishing, scuba diving, swimming, and windsurfing. The Indonesians particularly like boat-racing.

In addition to football, some favorite land sports include volleyball, golf, basketball, and badminton. The latter game is far more popular across Southeast Asia than it is in the United States. Like the Japanese, Koreans, and most other Asians, the residents of Southeast Asia are also devoted to martial arts, or combat sports. Many countries in the region have their own version or versions. Malaysia has its native *silat* (see-LAT), and Indonesia has a similar discipline called *pencak* (pen-CHAK) *silat*, Vietnam has *Vovinam*, and Thailand has *Muay Thai* (moy tie).

A kind of kickboxing, Muay Thai is several centuries old. Today, it is widely popular across the world, and many foreign martial arts styles incorporate some of its moves. Schools for the sport exist in Thailand and numerous other countries. One such school, run by the famous Muay Thai champion Chinnarach Chor Wattarin, is located on the Thai island of Koh Phangan. The school's website explains, "Muay Thai is referred to as 'The Science of Eight Limbs.'" This is because "the hands, shins, elbows, and knees are all used extensively in this art." The sport is "overflowing with color and ceremony." It also features exciting moments of "clenched-teeth action."[3]

From Snooker to *Star Trek*

Many of the other leisure activities that Southeast Asians enjoy are the same or similar to those popular in the West. Cambodians, Thais, Filipinos, and their neighbors like going out to dinner, for instance. They also enjoy playing video games and snooker (SNOOK-er). Similar to pool (or billiards), snooker was introduced to the region by the British in the 1800s.

Music concerts are also broadly attended. The various Southeast Asian peoples have their traditional ethnic music, in which people play ancient instruments. But almost everyone in the region enjoys Western music, too. Rock, pop, and hip-hop are widely popular.

Vietnam's Nguyen Thi Hang spars with Malaysia's Emy Latif in the Southeast Asian Games in November 2011. Their sport, pencak silat, is a popular martial art in the region.

Also like others around the world do, the locals sometimes sing along to their favorite songs in karaoke bars or cafés.

Going to the movies is another popular pastime in Southeast Asia. Big-budget American action and science fiction movies usually top the box office lists. And the *Star Trek* and *Star Wars* films have legions of Southeast Asian fans. Along with the popularity of soccer and other international sports in the region, this is revealing. It shows that the ancient cultures that grew up there have become part of the larger world culture as well.

Four girls enjoy a round of karaoke in their hometown of Manila, the capital and second-largest city in the Philippines. Karaoke is among the many Western entertainment pastimes that have become popular among young Southeast Asians.

"Go Indonesian Badminton!"

Badminton is widely popular in Southeast Asia. Many schools in the region have badminton teams. And Southeast Asian badminton players have won several international championships. One young Indonesian woman named Mahendrawathi Er blogs about the sport. She says her "love for badminton" started in childhood. "Both my grandpa and dad love watching it," she writes. "I remember watching the historic match in 1984" between Indonesia's Hastomo Arbi and China's Han Jian. Arbi won, which helped Indonesia regain badminton's biggest award—the Thomas Cup. "From then on" Mahendrawathi says, "I fell in love with the sport." She tells how in 1992, Indonesia made history. Its players Susi Susanti and Alan Budi Kusuma won the Olympic gold medal in the sport. Her country "finally joined selected countries that actually won Olympic gold." At the London Olympic Games, in 2012, however, the Indonesian badminton players did not win the gold. As a result, "our country was really in mourning." Yet "we still have high hopes" for doing better in the future. "After all, badminton is our national pride! Go Indonesian badminton!"[4]

The defending Indonesian badminton champion, Susi Susanti, displays an athletic stretch during the women's singles of the Japan Open, held in Tokyo in 1996. Susanti had won the tournament three times before, but lost this time.

Experiencing Southeast Asian Culture in the United States

You can experience Southeast Asian Culture right in your own neighborhood! Check out a cookbook with regional recipes, and try a few of them out in your kitchen. Or, sample some dishes at a local restaurant featuring Southeast Asian cuisine. Check out an online radio station, or talk to a friend or neighbor from that part of the world to find out more about their culture!

Restaurant Guides
The Ten Best Thai Restaurants in New York City
   http://blogs.villagevoice.com/forkintheroad/2013/10/
   the_10_best_thai_restaurants_nyc.php
Our Ten Best Vietnamese Restaurants (New York City)
   http://blogs.villagevoice.com/forkintheroad/2011/07/
   10_best_vietnamese_restaurants_in_new_york.php
Filipino Restaurants in Chicago
   http://traveltips.usatoday.com/filipino-restaurants-chicago-illinois-usa-61592.html

You can still try Southeast Asian food even if you don't live in a big city like New York or Chicago. Try a search for "Indonesian food," "Thai food," "Vietnamese food," or "Filipino food" in your neighborhood: http://www.yelp.com/

Museums
Asian Art at New York City's Metropolitan Museum of Art
   http://www.metmuseum.org/en/about-the-museum/museum-departments/
   curatorial-departments/asian-art
Islamic Art at New York City's Metropolitan Museum of Art
   http://www.metmuseum.org/about-the-museum/museum-departments/
   curatorial-departments/islamic-art
Southeast Asian Art at the Art Institute of Chicago
   http://www.artic.edu/aic/collections/artwork/category/105
South and Southeast Asian Art at the Boston Museum of Fine Arts
   http://www.mfa.org/collections/featured-galleries/south-and-southeast-asian-art

Online Radio Stations
Thai Radio Stations
   http://tunein.com/radio/Thailand-r101304/
Indonesian Music
   http://www.last.fm/tag/indonesia
Cambodian Radio
   http://www.khmerlive.tv/radio/

Cultural Organizations
Vietnam Learning, Arts & Cultural Center, New York City
   http://www.vlacc.org/
Indonesian Cultural Center of Pittsburgh
   http://icc-pgh.weebly.com/
Thai Cultural Center of the San Francisco Bay Area
   http://tccsfbayarea.org/
Philippine Cultural Foundation (Tampa, Florida)
   http://www.pcfitampa.org/
South-East Asia Center (Chicago)
   http://se-asiacenter.net/about.html

Map of Southeast Asia

TIMELINE

BCE

ca. 48,000   Humans live in the Tabon Caves of the modern-day Philippines.

ca. 3000   People in modern-day Thailand create bronze tools.

ca. 2879   Hung Vuong founds the first Vietnamese kingdom of Van Lang.

CE

700s   The Medang Kingdom is established on the Indonesian island of Java.

1100s   Angkor Wat is built as a Hindu temple in Cambodia; it is later used as a Buddhist temple instead.

1350   The Kingdom of Ayutthaya is established in Thailand.

1565   Spain founds a colony on Cebu Island in the Philippines.

1884   France invades Southeast Asia; by 1887 French Indochina is created, made up of Vietnam, Laos, and Cambodia.

1887   Prince Damrong of Siam (Thailand) becomes the Minister of Education and begins modernizing the country's education system.

1898   Spain cedes the Philippines to the United States.

1939   Siam is renamed Thailand.

1945   Vietnam declares its independence, which results in war with France.

1946   The United States grants the Philippines its independence.

1949   Indonesia gains its independence.

1954   The Vietnamese defeat the French and gain independence, but the country is divided into North Vietnam and South Vietnam.

1957   Malaysia gains its independence.

1963   The United States increases its military presence in Vietnam, teaming up with South Vietnam to fight North Vietnam in what Americans call the Vietnam War. (The Vietnamese call it the American War.)

1965   Singapore separates from Malaysia, becoming independent.

1973   After years of war, North Vietnam prevails, the Americans leave, and in 1975, the two Vietnams are reunited.

1984   Brunei gains independence from Britain.

1992   Indonesian badminton players win two gold medals at the summer Olympic Games.

1995   The United States and Vietnam establish normal relations.

1996   The Philippines and Malaysia jointly create the Turtle Islands Heritage Protected Area (TIHPA), designed to protect the habitats of endangered animal species.

2002   East Timor gains independence from Indonesia.

2004   An enormous tsunami strikes Southeast Asia, killing hundreds of thousands of people and causing widespread damage.

2013   Football fans in Myanmar riot after their national team loses to Indonesia.

2014   At the 2014 Winter Olympics, in Sochi, Russia, Michael Christian Martinez becomes the first Southeast Asian athlete ever to compete in the Olympic figure skating events.

CHAPTER NOTES

Introduction: A Region of Diversity and Dangers

1. *Jakarta Globe*, "Indonesia's Mount Merapi Volcano Erupts Again: Witnesses," October 30, 2010. http://www.thejakartaglobe.com/archive/indonesias-mount-merapi-volcano-erupts-again-witnesses/
2. BBC News: Asia-Pacific, "Indonesia Volcano Eruption Death Toll Hits 25," October 27, 2010. http://www.bbc.co.uk/news/world-asia-pacific-11633213
3. CIA, *The World Factbook*, "Indonesia." https://www.cia.gov/library/publications/the-world-factbook/geos/id.html
4. Sophie Brown, *Time*, "The Philippines Is the Most Storm-Exposed Country on Earth," November 11, 2013. http://world.time.com/2013/11/11/the-philippines-is-the-most-storm-exposed-country-on-earth/
5. Jennifer Preston, *New York Times* blog, *The Lede*, "Eyewitness Reports After Typhoon in Philippines," November 8, 2013. http://thelede.blogs.nytimes.com/2013/11/08/eyewitness-reports-after-typhoon-in-philippines/?_r=0
6. Kalikasan, "Where Are the Trees? Examining the State of the Philippine Forests." http://www.kalikasan.net/features/2011/06/05/where-are-trees-examining-state-philippine-forests

Chapter 1: An Unforgettable Shared Experience

1. *AsianConnections.com*, "Tsunami Disaster Eyewitness Account." http://www.asianconnections.com/a/?article_id=566
2. Catherine Wentworth, *A Woman Learning Thai*, "Remembering Tsunami 2004: And Then One Morning," December 26, 2010. http://womenlearnthai.com/index.php/tsunami-2004-and-then-one-morning/
3. *Wild Asia*, "Malaysian Tourism After the Tsunami Aftermath," March 30, 2005. http://www.wildasia.org/main.cfm/library/Malaysia_recovers_from_tsunami
4. James Borton, *Asia Times*, "Tsunami Bloggers in Tribal News Network," 2005. http://www.atimes.com/atimes/Southeast_Asia/GA05Ae02.html

5. Ibid.
6. Ibid.
7. SEA-EAT Blog, "To Our Readers." http://tsunamihelp.blogspot.com/2005/01/to-our-readers.html#110682988047344329

Chapter 2: Family, Marriage, and the Home

1. Graham Colin-Jones and Yvonne Colin-Jones, *Philippines: A Quick Guide to Customs and Etiquette* (London: Kuperard, 2004), p. 46.
2. Trang Nguyen, Vietnamese American Oral History Project, UC Irvine, "Oral History of Dan The Le," April 28, 2012. http://ucispace.lib.uci.edu/bitstream/handle/10575/2088/VAOHP0040.2,"_F01.pdf?sequence=7
3. Trang Nguyen, Vietnamese American Oral History Project, UC Irvine, "Oral History of Dan The Le," April 21 and April 28, 2012. http://ucispace.lib.uci.edu/bitstream/handle/10575/2088/VAOHP0040.1_F01.pdf?sequence=6
4. Samantha Erica Takahashi, Vietnamese American Oral History Project, UC Irvine, "Oral History of Alex Thai Nguyen," February 10, 2013. http://ucispace.lib.uci.edu/bitstream/handle/10575/8401/VAOHP0111_F01.pdf?sequence=2
5. Trang Nguyen, Vietnamese American Oral History Project, UC Irvine, "Oral History of Dan The Le," April 21 and April 28, 2012. http://ucispace.lib.uci.edu/bitstream/handle/10575/2088/VAOHP0040.1_F01.pdf?sequence=6

Chapter 3: A Fantastic Mix of Faiths and Beliefs

1. Jochen Schlingmann, *Asienreisender*, "Southeast Asia," April 26, 2012. http://www.asienreisender.de/southeastasia.html
2. Ajaan Lee Dhammadharo, translated by Thanissaro Bhikkhu, *Access to Insight*, "The Path to Peace and Freedom for the Mind," December 1, 2013. http://www.accesstoinsight.org/lib/thai/lee/pathtopeace.html

CHAPTER NOTES

3. Figure is estimated based on population data from CIA, *The World Factbook*, "Indonesia," https://www.cia.gov/library/publications/the-world-factbook/geos/id.html, and annual population growth rate from The World Bank, "Population Growth (Annual %)," http://data.worldbank.org/indicator/SP.POP.GROW

4. Tom Verde, interview with Parag Khanna, *Saudi Aramco World*, "The Multipolar Future," May/June 2011, pp. 40-43. http://www.saudiaramcoworld.com/issue/201103/the.multipolar.future.htm

5. Tahmena Bokhari, *History of Islam across Muslim Villages of Southeast Asia*, "Origins of Islam," May 5, 2007. http://tahmenabokharisoutheastasia.blogspot.com/

6. Pew Research Center, *The World's Muslims: Unity and Diversity*, August 9, 2012, p. 67. http://www.pewforum.org/files/2012/08/the-worlds-muslims-full-report.pdf

Chapter 4: Vanishing Animals and Rainforests

1. Sumatran Orangutan Society, "Baby Orangutan Rescued from Illegal Pet Trade in Sumatra," May 28, 2013. http://orangutans-sos.org/news/446_baby-orangutan-rescued-from-illegal-pet-trade-in-sumatra

2. Ibid.

3. WWF-Malaysia, "Forests." http://www.wwf.org.my/about_wwf/what_we_do/forests_main/

4. Kalikasan, "Where Are the Trees? Examining the State of the Philippine Forests." http://www.kalikasan.net/features/2011/06/05/where-are-trees-examining-state-philippine-forests

5. Projected from Earth Snapshot, "Climate Change and Deforestation in the Philippines," May 22, 2013. http://www.eosnap.com/image-of-the-day/climate-change-and-deforestation-in-the-philippines-may-22nd-2013/

6. Michael Sullivan, NPR, "As China Builds, Cambodia's Forests Fall," January 29, 2013. http://www.npr.org/2013/01/29/170580214/as-china-builds-cambodias-forests-fall

7. Kalikasan, "Where Are the Trees? Examining the State of the Philippine Forests." http://www.kalikasan.net/features/2011/06/05/where-are-trees-examining-state-philippine-forests

8. This date is the author's estimation based on information from this article: Michael Sullivan, NPR, "As China Builds, Cambodia's Forests Fall," January 29, 2013. http://www.npr.org/2013/01/29/170580214/as-china-builds-cambodias-forests-fall

Chapter 5: Common Foods and Dining Customs

1. Joyce Jue, *Savoring Southeast Asia* (San Francisco: Weldon Owen, 2000), p. 16.

2. Luke Nguyen, *Luke Nguyen's Greater Mekong*, "Pork Grilled in Bamboo." https://cooked.com.au/Luke-Nguyen/Hardie-Grant-Books/Luke-Nguyens-Greater-Mekong/Thailand/Pork-chargrilled-in-bamboo-recipe

3. Kiran Tarun, "Pandan Kaya," July 19, 2013. http://kirantarun.com/food/2013/07/19/pandan-kaya-coconut-screwpine-jam/

4. Luke Nguyen, "Cambodia." https://cooked.com.au/Luke-Nguyen/publisher/Luke-Nguyens-Greater-Mekong/Cambodia

5. Alfred Russel Wallace, "On the Bamboo and Durian of Borneo," 1856. http://people.wku.edu/charles.smith/wallace/S027.htm

Chapter 6: Sports and Other Leisure Activities

1. *The National*, "Riots Follow Myanmar Football Exit from Southeast Asian Games," December 17, 2013. http://www.thenational.ae/sport/football/riots-follow-myanmar-football-exit-from-southeast-asian-games

2. Mong Palatino, *GlobalVoices*, "Southeast Asia: Blogging about Football," September 27, 2010. http://globalvoicesonline.org/2010/09/27/southeast-asia-blogging-about-football/

3. Muay Thai Chinnarach. http://www.muaythaichinnarach.com/

4. Mahendrawathi Er, *The M Ways*, "Why Indonesia Loves Badminton!" June 16, 2013. http://mwe4eva.wordpress.com/2013/06/16/why-indonesia-loves-badminton/

FURTHER READING

Books

Gitlin, Martin. *Vietnam War.* Minneapolis: Essential Library, 2013.

Goodman, Jim, and Michael Spilling. *Thailand.* Terrytown, NY: Marshall Cavendish, 2012.

Hoyer, Daniel. *Culinary Vietnam.* Layton, UT: Gibbs Smith, 2009.

Koh, Jamie. *Singapore Childhood: Our Stories, Then and Now.* Singapore: World Scientific Publishing, 2013.

Munan, Heidi, et al. *Malaysia.* Terrytown, NY: Marshall Cavendish, 2012.

Nardo, Don. *Buddhism.* Mankato, MN: Compass Point Books, 2010.

Nicolai, Gregory. *Teens in Vietnam.* Mankato, MN: Compass Point Books, 2007.

Spilsbury, Louise. *Indonesia and Jakarta.* New York: Franklin Watts, 2014.

Yuson, Alfred A., and George Tapan. *The Philippines: Islands of Enchantment.* North Clarendon, VT: Tuttle Publishing, 2003.

On the Internet

Buddhism for Teenagers
  http://dhammadana.fr/en.htm

National Geographic: "Philippines"
  http://travel.nationalgeographic.com/travel/countries/philippines-guide/

NewScientist: "Biodiversity Wipeout Facing Southeast Asia"
  http://www.newscientist.com/article/dn3973#.UsWrLrR0n0m

Time for Kids: "Indonesia"
  http://www.timeforkids.com/destination/indonesia

Tsunami 2004
  http://www.tsunami2004.net/

Works Consulted

AsianConnections.com. "Tsunami Disaster Eyewitness Account."
  http://www.asianconnections.com/a/?article_id=566

Baker, Chris, and Pasuk Phongpaichit. *A History of Thailand.* New York: Cambridge University Press, 2009.

BBC News: Asia-Pacific. "Indonesia Volcano Eruption Death Toll Hits 25." October 27, 2010. http://www.bbc.co.uk/news/world-asia-pacific-11633213

Bokhari, Tahmena. "Origins of Islam." *History of Islam across Muslim Villages of Southeast Asia,* May 5, 2007. http://tahmenabokharisoutheastasia.blogspot.com/

Borton, James. "Tsunami Bloggers in Tribal News Network." *Asia Times,* 2005.
  http://www.atimes.com/atimes/Southeast_Asia/GA05Ae02.html

Bray, Adam, and Mark Beales. *Vietnam.* London: Insight Guides, 2012.

Bray, Adam, et al. *Laos and Cambodia.* London: Insight Guides, 2013.

Brown, Sophie. "The Philippines Is the Most Storm-Exposed Country on Earth." *Time,* November 11, 2013. http://world.time.com/2013/11/11/the-philippines-is-the-most-storm-exposed-country-on-earth/

CaoDai.org. http://www.caodai.org/web/content.aspx?pageID=1

CIA. *The World Factbook.* https://www.cia.gov/library/publications/the-world-factbook/

Colin-Jones, Graham, and Yvonne Colin-Jones. *Philippines: A Quick Guide to Customs and Etiquette.* London: Kuperard, 2004.

Dayley, Robert, and Clark D. Neher. *Southeast Asia in the New International Era.* Boulder, CO: Westview Press, 2013.

Dhammadharo, Ajaan Lee. Translated by Thanissaro Bhikkhu. "The Path to Peace and Freedom for the Mind." *Access to Insight,* December 1, 2013. http://www.accesstoinsight.org/lib/thai/lee/pathtopeace.html

59

FURTHER READING

Earth Snapshot. "Climate Change and Deforestation in the Philippines." May 22, 2013. http://www.eosnap.com/image-of-the-day/climate-change-and-deforestation-in-the-philippines-may-22nd-2013/

Er, Mahendrawathi. "Why Indonesia Loves Badminton!" *The M Ways*, June 16, 2013. http://mwe4eva.wordpress.com/2013/06/16/why-indonesia-loves-badminton/

Francia, Luis H. *A History of the Philippines*. New York: Overlook, 2010.

Hellwig, Tineke, and Eric Tagliacozzo, eds. *The Indonesia Reader*. Durham, NC: Duke University Press, 2009.

Jakarta Globe. "Indonesia's Mount Merapi Volcano Erupts Again: Witnesses." October 30, 2010. http://www.thejakartaglobe.com/archive/indonesias-mount-merapi-volcano-erupts-again-witnesses/

Jennings, Ralph. *Philippines*. London: Insight Guides, 2013.

Jianxin, Wang, and Zhang Yongxing. "Singapore Plays Active Role in Tsunami Relief Efforts." Reliefweb, January 17, 2005. http://img.static.reliefweb.int/report/myanmar/singapore-plays-active-role-tsunami-relief-efforts

Jue, Joyce. *Savoring Southeast Asia*. San Francisco: Weldon Owen, 2000.

Kalikasan. "Where Are the Trees? Examining the State of the Philippine Forests." http://www.kalikasan.net/features/2011/06/05/where-are-trees-examining-state-philippine-forests

Karber, Phil. *The Indochina Chronicles: Travels in Laos, Cambodia and Vietnam*. Singapore: Marshall Cavendish International Asia, 2012.

Lockard, Craig A. *Southeast Asia in World History*. New York: Oxford University Press, 2009.

Mahmood, Datuk Dr Jemilah, et. al. "Annual Report 2005." Mercy Malaysia. http://www.mercy.org.my/upload/MERCY%20Malaysia%20Annual%20Report%202005.pdf

Muay Thai Chinnarach. http://www.muaythaichinnarach.com/

The National. "Riots Follow Myanmar Football Exit from Southeast Asian Games." December 17, 2013. http://www.thenational.ae/sport/football/riots-follow-myanmar-football-exit-from-southeast-asian-games

Nguyen, Luke. "Cambodia." https://cooked.com.au/Luke-Nguyen/publisher/Luke-Nguyens-Greater-Mekong/Cambodia

Nguyen, Luke. "Pork Grilled in Bamboo." *Luke Nguyen's Greater Mekong*. https://cooked.com.au/Luke-Nguyen/Hardie-Grant-Books/Luke-Nguyens-Greater-Mekong/Thailand/Pork-chargrilled-in-bamboo-recipe

Nguyen, Trang. "Oral History of Dan The Le." Vietnamese American Oral History Project, UC Irvine, April 21 and April 28, 2012. http://ucispace.lib.uci.edu/bitstream/handle/10575/2088/VAOHP0040.1_F01.pdf?sequence=6

Nguyen, Trang. "Oral History of Dan The Le." Vietnamese American Oral History Project, UC Irvine, April 28, 2012. http://ucispace.lib.uci.edu/bitstream/handle/10575/2088/VAOHP0040.2,"_F01.pdf?sequence=7

Osborne, Milton. *Southeast Asia: An Introductory History*. Crows Nest, Australia: Allen and Unwin, 2013.

Pacific Disaster Management Information Network. "Indian Ocean Earthquake & Tsunami Emergency Update." January 1, 2005. http://www.who.int/hac/crises/idn/sitreps/en/Asian%20Tsunami%20HAR%20010105.pdf

Palatino, Mong. "Southeast Asia: Blogging about Football." *GlobalVoices*, September 27, 2010. http://globalvoicesonline.org/2010/09/27/southeast-asia-blogging-about-football/

Pew Research Center. *The World's Muslims: Unity and Diversity*. August 9, 2012. http://www.pewforum.org/files/2012/08/the-worlds-muslims-full-report.pdf

FURTHER READING

Preston, Jennifer. "Eyewitness Reports After Typhoon in Philippines." *New York Times* blog, *The Lede*, November 8, 2013. http://thelede.blogs.nytimes.com/2013/11/08/eyewitness-reports-after-typhoon-in-philippines/?_r=0

Ranges, Trevor. *National Geographic Traveler: Cambodia.* Washington, DC: National Geographic, 2010.

Richardson, Howard. *Thailand.* London: Insight Guides, 2013.

Salter, Christopher L. *South and East Asia and the Pacific.* New York: Holt, Rinehart, and Winston, 2009.

SarDesai, D. R. *Southeast Asia: Past and Present.* Boulder, CO: Westview Press, 2013.

Schlingmann, Jochen. "Southeast Asia." *Asienreisender*, April 26, 2012. http://www.asienreisender.de/southeastasia.html

SEA-EAT Blog. "To Our Readers." http://tsunamihelp.blogspot.com/2005/01/to-our-readers.html#110682988047344329

Sullivan, Michael. "As China Builds, Cambodia's Forests Fall." NPR, January 29, 2013. http://www.npr.org/2013/01/29/170580214/as-china-builds-cambodias-forests-fall

Sumatran Orangutan Society. "Baby Orangutan Rescued from Illegal Pet Trade in Sumatra." May 28, 2013. http://orangutans-sos.org/news/446_baby-orangutan-rescued-from-illegal-pet-trade-in-sumatra

Takahashi, Samantha Erica. "Oral History of Alex Thai Nguyen." Vietnamese American Oral History Project, UC Irvine, February 10, 2013. http://ucispace.lib.uci.edu/bitstream/handle/10575/8401/VAOHP0111_F01.pdf?sequence=2

Tan, Terry, and Vilma Laus. *Best-Ever Cooking of Malaysia, Singapore, Indonesia, & the Philippines.* London: Southwater, 2014.

Tarun, Kiran. "Pandan Kaya." July 19, 2013. http://kirantarun.com/food/2013/07/19/pandan-kaya-coconut-screwpine-jam/

Tully, John. *A Short History of Cambodia.* Crows Nest, Australia: Allen and Unwin, 2005.

Vatikiotis, Michael. *Indonesia: Islands of the Imagination.* North Clarendon, VT: Tuttle Publishing, 2006.

Verde, Tom. Interview with Parag Khanna. "The Multipolar Future." *Saudi Aramco World*, May/June 2011, pp. 40–43. http://www.saudiaramcoworld.com/issue/201103/the.multipolar.future.htm

Wallace, Alfred Russel. "On the Bamboo and Durian of Borneo." 1856. http://people.wku.edu/charles.smith/wallace/S027.htm

Watson, C. W., and Roy Ellen, eds. *Understanding Witchcraft and Sorcery in Southeast Asia.* Honolulu: University of Hawaii Press, 1993.

Weightman, Barbara A. *Dragons and Tigers: A Geography of South, East and Southeast Asia.* Oxford, UK: Wiley, 2011.

Wentworth, Catherine. "Remembering Tsunami 2004: And Then One Morning." *A Woman Learning Thai*, December 26, 2010. http://womenlearnthai.com/index.php/tsunami-2004-and-then-one-morning/

Wild Asia. "Malaysian Tourism After the Tsunami Aftermath." March 30, 2005. http://www.wildasia.org/main.cfm/library/Malaysia_recovers_from_tsunami

Wong, Siew Lyn, and HonYuen Leong. *Malaysia.* London: Insight Guides, 2013.

World Bank. "Population Growth (Annual %)." http://data.worldbank.org/indicator/SP.POP.GROW

WWF-Malaysia. "Forests." http://www.wwf.org.my/about_wwf/what_we_do/forests_main/

GLOSSARY

activist (AK-tuh-vist)—A person who avidly works either to change or defend a social, political, or economic rule or norm.

arranged marriage—A union of a bride and groom that results from an agreement worked out by their parents or some other relatives.

backhoe (BAK-hoh)—A machine with a large bucket used for digging big holes or clearing land.

blog—An online journal or diary.

deforestation (dee-fawr-ist-AY-shuhn)—The destruction or clearing of forests or trees.

extinction (ik-STINGK-shuhn)—The complete and permanent elimination of a plant or animal species.

habitat—The area in the wild in which a kind of animal naturally lives.

karaoke (kar-ee-OH-kee)—An act of singing along with prerecorded popular songs into a microphone.

machete (muh-SHET-ee)—A long knife with a wide blade used for cutting crops and forest plants.

sacrifice—To give up something for something else of higher value.

species—A specific kind of animal, plant, or other life form.

stilts—Poles that hold something up, such as a house.

wok—A large frying pan shaped like a bowl, commonly used in Asian cooking.

INDEX

About the Author

Historian and award-winning writer Don Nardo has published more than four hundred books for teens and children, along with a number of volumes for college and general adult readers. Although his specialty is the ancient world, he has written about the medieval and modern eras as well, including studies of the history and culture of peoples and nations across the world. Mr. Nardo, who also composes and arranges orchestral music, lives with his wife, Christine, in Massachusetts.